This book belongs to

....

For the next generation of gardeners—C.D.

For my grandad, who taught my mum,
who taught me the love of growing my own—K.L.

Published in 2023 by Welbeck Editions
An imprint of Welbeck Children's Limited,
part of Welbeck Publishing Group.
Based in London and Sydney.
www.welbeckpublishing.com

Design and layout © Welbeck Children's Limited 2023
Text © 2023 Charles Dowding
Illustrations © 2023 Kristyna Litten

978 1 78312 919 5

Printed in Heshan, China

9 8 7 6 5 4 3 2

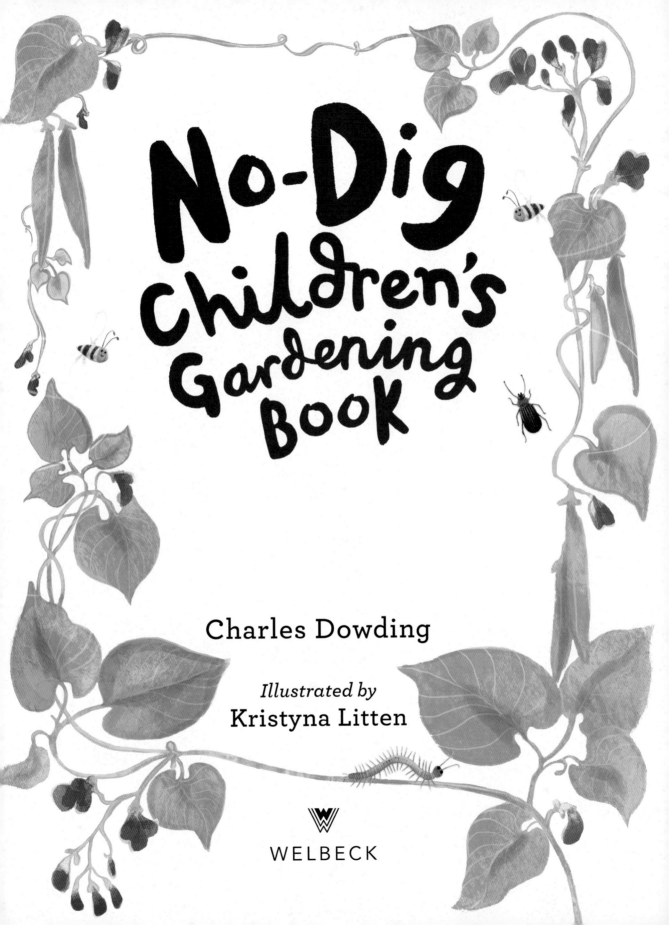

No-Dig
Children's
Gardening
Book

Charles Dowding

Illustrated by
Kristyna Litten

WELBECK

Contents

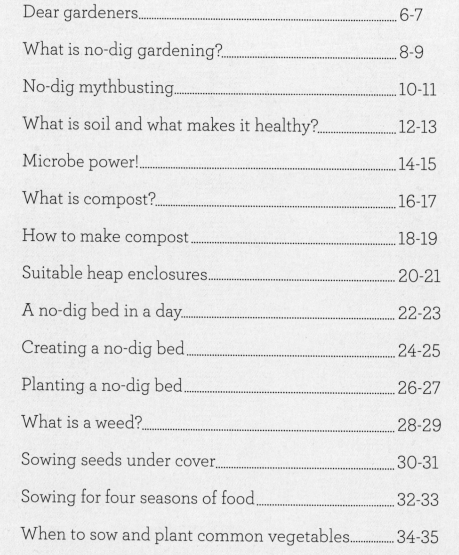

Dear gardeners (big and small)

Welcome to the wonderful world of no-dig gardening.

Let this book inspire you and help you to make a no-dig bed. Discover for yourself how simple and quick it is. Then watch how your plants grow, and how good they taste.

No-dig is easy and it makes sense. We work with nature which means that she doesn't fight back with weeds. You don't have to do much weeding. You can enjoy sowing, growing, and picking. No-dig copies nature's way of feeding plants through the soil. All we need to do is cover the surface and allow the process to happen.

Watch your plants grow and feel your own knowledge and happiness growing at the same time. Big or small, there's so much you can do together in a garden, and at any time of the year.

Enjoy!

Charles Dowding

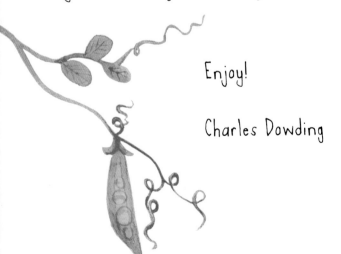

What is no-dig gardening?

No-dig is simple. And if something's simple, it's great to do with kids! This is the essence of no-dig gardening in two steps. Once you understand them, you can go and do it! The rest of this book explains materials to use, best ways to use them, and at what time of year. And the best thing is, you can make a no-dig bed in any month.

So how is something so simple, also so good for your garden? It's because it allows nature to work with us. She wants plants to grow as much as we do. This knowledge is liberating because it reveals how we don't need to work hard at digging, among many other unnecessary jobs that until now have been done by so many gardeners.

No-dig may be trickier to get to grips with for experienced gardeners because it means they need to unlearn what they thought was correct knowledge. Luckily, kids don't have these preconceived ideas about gardening, so no-dig is the perfect way to get them into gardening. We all learn a lot outside the classroom, and gardening teaches us so much, whatever our age!

Step 1: Any soil which is already growing plants has a good structure for new plantings. The plants growing in your garden at the moment may well be what we call weeds, and with no-dig you simply cover the weeds with something that stops light from reaching their leaves. That process is called mulching. An excellent material to use for mulching is common old cardboard, matte not shiny and with tape removed.

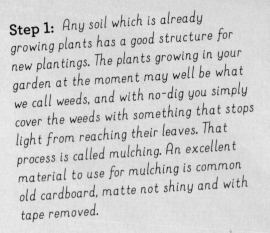

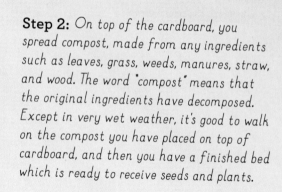

Step 2: On top of the cardboard, you spread compost, made from any ingredients such as leaves, grass, weeds, manures, straw, and wood. The word "compost" means that the original ingredients have decomposed. Except in very wet weather, it's good to walk on the compost you have placed on top of cardboard, and then you have a finished bed which is ready to receive seeds and plants.

No-dig mythbusting

Children don't have preconceptions about what is right and wrong, in terms of preparing ground for plants. But adults often do! So here is some myth busting to set the record straight.

MYTH: *Soil and compost should be loose and crumbly for new plantings.*

FACT: Firm soil is good. We have valuable coworkers in the soil, and no-dig allows them to get on with their important jobs. Some are visible—such as earthworms and millipedes, toads and beetles. Many are not visible, such as thin threads of fungi whose old skins help to glue soil particles together. As the soil's inhabitants move around, they keep soil open and aerated. They can move easily and freely in the stable structure of no-dig soil, which contains air channels. Air is important in soil because some organisms need the oxygen, and it means that water can filter down, while plant roots also can travel more freely.

MYTH: *Digging the soil will help introduce this all-important air.*

FACT: People think that by digging the soil they are allowing air to enter, and indeed this happens for a few weeks. However, the soil then slumps down because digging has broken up its structure. Digging does the opposite to what many think. It's a lose-lose process where people get locked onto a treadmill of having to do it regularly.

MYTH: *Compost burns plant roots.*

FACT: Seeds and plants grow well in all mature compost, which does not need to be mixed with or into soil. Damage happens only if people make the mistake of planting into compost which is fresh, spread recently from a heap which was hot and steaming.

MYTH: Compost needs to be mixed into where roots will grow.

FACT: Soil and plants are healthiest when all the organic matter (compost) we apply is simply spread on the surface. The organisms in the soil instinctively expect it to be there, and they come up close to the surface to keep eating and excreting, building fertility all the time. You can find little white plant roots in the compost above soil, when it's damp.

MYTH: Digging soil means we can bury the weeds.

FACT: You can mulch with cardboard and compost to bury weeds, if there are a lot. After that it's quick to pull weeds because there are so few with the no-dig method. Weed growth is partly a way that soil heals itself if it is disturbed. There is a lot of life in your soil and weed roots help this to thrive if the soil structure has been damaged through digging. There are microbes and fungi in soil which want to team up with plant roots. They help plants to grow and, in return, plants give them the food they need. That process is called mutual symbiosis and, for us, it's a win-win. We work less, plants grow more!

MYTH: Well, digging isn't going to do any harm, is it?

FACT: Not true! Another losing aspect of digging is that every time it's done, carbon is released into the air as carbon dioxide. Not only does this cause more climate change, but the carbon is lost from the soil, where it plays such a valuable role. Carbon in soil is the building block of all organic matter, the food for all life. It's absolutely vital—and a great source of carbon is the compost we place on top.

What is soil and what makes it healthy?

Have you ever thought of soil as being alive? It's self organized and healing where necessary, growing plants above all, from trees and bushes to vegetables and weeds. Soil is the powerful, amazing interface between our atmosphere and the rocks below.

Soil profile

If you could see the soil beneath your feet, you would notice that it is made up of three main layers, each a slightly different color.

Step 1: *The dark surface is topsoil and that's where most of the life is. It's the part of soil we can easily change, by feeding its inhabitants. With no-dig we improve soil's ability to grow healthy plants, and nourish us.*

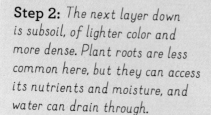

Step 2: *The next layer down is subsoil, of lighter color and more dense. Plant roots are less common here, but they can access its nutrients and moisture, and water can drain through.*

Step 3: *Below the subsoil is rock or broken stone, sometimes gravel or boulders, depending what happened long ago in your location. Geologists study this zone and its bodies of old organisms rather than living ones.*

Soil life and health

What might soil be like under a city? Look at how trees grow out of
pavements, their roots strong enough to push up the stone and concrete.
There is still life in the soil underneath, which I find impressive and reassuring.

Variations in soil include depth, color, ability to hold food and moisture, and the life
that lives there. Organisms range from ones we see, like earthworms and centipedes,
to invisible ones like bacteria and fungal spores. Soil networks of life are the key to
plants growing. The world's top soil microbiologist, Dr. Elaine Ingham from Oregon,
says that all soils have enough food for plants, but the roots may not be able to access
it unless soil is fully alive.

Imagine soil as our planet's skin. When healthy, it's protected by surface layers
of organic matter, and is full of roots which helps the biology to work well. With
no-dig, we maintain a thin layer of compost over the soil to absorb rainwater
like a sponge, keep moisture in when it's hot, and feed the life.

Microbe power!

Microbes are invisible and it's easy to ignore them, yet they are the soil's "engine of moving parts." They make everything work and they help your plants to grow.

The word microbe is descriptive of tiny size. It is not a scientific term. Here I use it to include what my mother called "germs," such as bacteria, fungi, and protozoa. The population of microbes and how they interact at any one time is a key factor for soil structure and health.

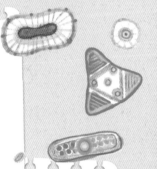

Protozoa, for example, are microscopic single cell animals which feed on organic matter, such as other microorganisms. One type, called diatoms, look like mini cucumbers when under a microscope. One thing they do is to convert dissolved carbon dioxide into oxygen and this improves soil for other organisms. Diatoms are most numerous in soils which are not dug.

The health of all organisms comes from a balance of busy microbes. Our bodies, for example, host billions of microbes, all eating and excreting. Much of this happens in our guts, where we need a high population of microbes to help digest our food. Gut microbes are very similar to those found in soil, which is why it's healthy to eat a little soil, say after you pull a carrot and don't wash it too clean before eating! Gardeners tend to be happy people. I think it's because they're picking up microbes from soil and plants, such as *Bacillum vacca*, which help to produce the feel-good hormone called serotonin.

Microbial balance happens in soil when there is enough air, moisture, and decomposing or decomposed organic matter. No-dig ensures all of this because we are feeding the microbes with compost and organic matter, without disturbing them.

Take a look at some soil to help you understand how much is going on there. Use a trowel to lift some out of a small hole, and while I know this is not no-dig, it is okay to do this occasionally!

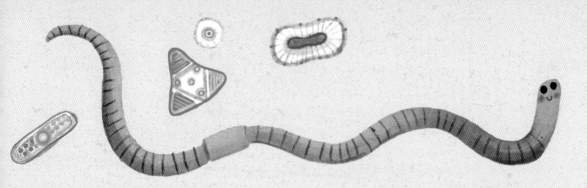

I find the most amazing inhabitant of soil is the earthworm, *Lumbricus terrestris*. You find them in topsoil almost everywhere, because they do the most recycling of decaying plant matter such as old leaves, and turn them into food for plants. You can see this on the surface of many lawns, where the grass being short means we can see spirals of soil-like material. They are the excretions of earthworms called casts, and they contain a fantastic amount of plant nutrients.

The other common worm type is *Eisenia fetida*, called many names such as red tiger, brandling, or fishermans' worm because you can use them as bait to attract fish. Their color is bright red and they are thinner and shorter than earthworms. You see most of them in semi-decomposed plant matter such as the outer leaves of cabbage heads that are starting to rot, and they are used to convert organic matter into amazing worm compost. They squirm in a lively way when you touch them and appear in unlikely places. I even find them in the gutters of my greenhouse!

Another common organism is *Oniscus asellus*, usually called the common woodlouse. They are ancient crustaceans, related to crabs and shrimps, that eat and help to decompose any old woody material which is on the way to becoming soil.

To find out more you can use a microscope or a magnifying glass to reveal soil's universe of life and complexity. I find it reassuring that so much is happening, without any intervention from us. We should always encourage this to thrive.

What is compost?

Compost is any material which was once alive, and is now decomposed. Making compost in a heap is a great way to speed up the natural process of converting dead matter into valuable material. You can recycle all wastes of organic matter and then grow bigger, healthier plants.

Common ingredients of garden compost include leaves, grass, weeds, dead flowers, vegetables, and harvested vegetable plants. If you own a pet rabbit, hamster, or bird, you can also add their old bedding and droppings to the heap. You can also add cardboard packaging, with the tape removed and food waste, such as eggshells.

How nature does it

When you look at how decomposition works in fields and forests, you don't find any compost heaps! You see old organic matter lying on top, and then soil inhabitants such as earthworms come up to eat it close to the surface, or they take it down and eat it in the soil. Look closely under a garden tree, where in moist conditions you often see old tree leaves disappearing into the soil, in a slightly corkscrew fashion. This is from earthworms pulling them down into their burrows. Our compost heaps speed up the process of converting waste to food, we use it in the most natural way. All compost is simply spread on top, which is where soil organisms know to come and eat new food.

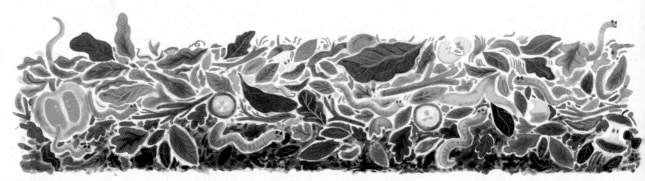

Imperfect, but the key to life

Compost often does not look perfect, and that is absolutely fine. It may be lumpy and uneven, with bits of wood, eggshell, and chicken bones still recognizable, but it always contains a lot of life, both visible and invisible.

Carbon is a vital ingredient for the soil. It can absorb and hold a lot of carbon and when it does that, there is plenty of food for the soil populations to eat. Food is available for the plant roots when they need it for growth, and there is plenty of air and moisture.

Compost heaps themselves are a valuable habitat for life of all sizes, from bacteria and insects to slow worms and frogs. I put a glass side on one of my compost heaps, by replacing the pallet with a large old window. I wanted to see what was happening inside there, but I saw less than I had hoped because most of the action happened in the middle where it was warmer. I did see some worms, and the green material turning to brown.

How to make compost

"All muck and magic" is an old phrase used for gardening, referring to how beautiful plants grow out of muck and dirt. We could also use it for the process of making compost, which is "muck into magic." We convert our garden waste into food for plants. Making compost is great for the planet too because it keeps the carbon locked into the soil ready for the plants to use.

What's good to add?

People often make this more complicated than necessary with lots of rules about what you can and can't add. In fact it's very simple. You can add anything that was once growing in a garden, a body, a field, or a forest. For example, you can add human and pet hair, sheep's wool, dust, eggshells, cardboard and paper (which is made from trees), straw, leaves, and weeds. But avoid adding materials like plastic, glossy paper (which has a chemical coating), or metal because your composting organisms will not be able to eat them.

Beware of adding anything that is described as "biodegradable." These items do degrade but they do not decompose. They just turn into smaller pieces of plastic! Items that are "compostable" will be fine to add. Check the packaging to see if you can add an item to your compost heap.

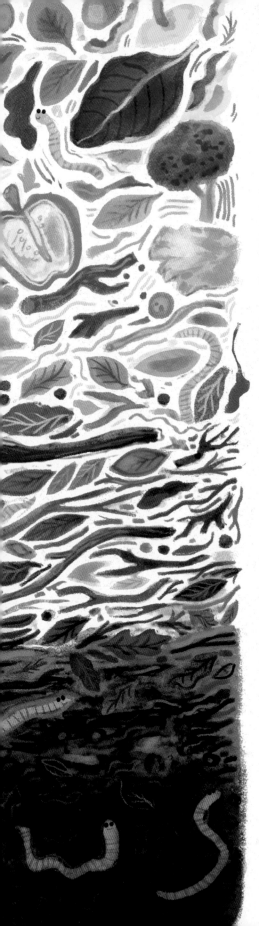

How to add materials

If you only ever add small amounts at a time, you don't need to organize how you add things to your heap. If you add a large amount at once, it is best to do this in layers of green waste, then brown waste. Green waste (flowers and leaves etc.) should be in layers of 3–4 in. with layers of brown waste (twigs or branches etc.) about 1–2 in. deep. Some green waste, like grass cuttings, slump into a soggy mass if you don't add brown waste to help hold the structure.

Brown waste has woody fibers which hold more space and air between them, and allows excess water to drain, and they decompose more slowly. They also promote the growth of fungi and keep the bacteria balanced which helps the whole composting process. Red brandling worms arrive in the final stages of decomposition. You can also keep these in trays in the garden shed where they will make small amounts of compost from paper and kitchen scraps.

You need a lot of raw materials to make a small amount of compost. Don't be discouraged by this and take it as an opportunity for foraging missions around your home and school to find other people's garden waste and add them to your heaps. They will be grateful to be rid of it and you'll enjoy a great result.

Suitable heap enclosures

You can buy ready-made bins of plastic or wooden materials. For small gardens, the beehive types work well because they are light enough to move to a new location if you wish. For larger gardens you will have more waste than can fit into one of these. It's worth making your own heaps using old pallets. I simply bind these to each other with just two pieces of wire at top and bottom. You will need eight pieces of wire, each about 18 in. long, and two people to hold the pallets while the third person secures the wires.

The perfect place

You may come across a lot of precise advice about where you should put your compost heap. I've read that they must be in the sun to get warm, or they must be in the shade to retain moisture. Both statements are nonsense and heaps can be wherever works best for your gardening. Put them somewhere central which makes it quick and easy to fill up. They are a beautiful addition to any garden and something to be proud of. Don't hide them away in a corner!

How many do I need?

The most manageable option is to have two heaps, so that while the first one is maturing you can be adding materials to the second one. You could also add a third bin, into which you can turn the almost-ready composting materials from the other two heaps. Then you always have space for new waste and a pile of compost ready for use.

Does a heap have to get hot?

The answer is no. However, if you add sufficient material over a period of a few days and at least half of this material is green, heat will occur. Heat kills weed seeds, and will speed up the composting process. I love to see steam rising from a heap on a cool morning. You can increase the temperature of a heap by lining the inside with cardboard, which holds in warmth, keeps moisture in, and stops the edges from drying out.

Is watering necessary?

In a damp climate, you almost never need to add water for making compost. There is plenty of moisture already in green leaves and the only time I add water is in very dry summers when green leaves aren't as moist as usual. Use a watering can with a fine rose to enable small droplets of water to scatter across the heap, rather than watering in one spot.

What does "turning" mean?

"Turning" means moving with a garden fork to break up lumps, introduce air, and to mix up materials that are decomposing at different speeds. I recommend it, and it's fun to do because it's a step back in time to see how everything you added has changed. You can make nice compost without turning, but it's worthwhile to do it if you can.

When is it ready to use?

Finished or mature compost can be anything from slightly lumpy and fibrous, to quite fine and soft. It's good to use at any point in the process. Apply lumpy compost before winter, so that weather can open and soften it, making it perfect for spring planting. If you are spreading compost just before sowing seeds or planting out seedlings, use finer compost. One thing you never need to do is to sieve it. That can damage the soil's microbes. It doesn't need to look perfect —woody bits in your compost make great food for fungi, and it's rare that they are fully decomposed when you are spreading. Remember that the materials decompose at different rates and that process is happening all the time, regardless of whether the compost is in a heap or a bed.

A no-dig bed in a day
Charles Dowding at Homeacres

One day in August, I arranged for a group of children to come along and help make a new bed at Homeacres. I had the cardboard and compost ready. They brought a couple of small wheelbarrows—and plenty of enthusiasm.

Preparation

Before the children arrived, I measured up the area of the new bed and laid some wooden planks to act as temporary sides. On the outside of each plank I banged in some wooden battens to hold the sides in place.

Mulching

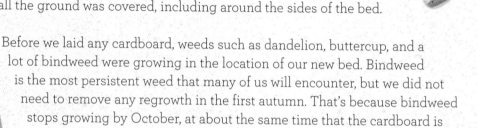

In the morning, we laid cardboard on the bed, making sure all edges were overlapping. We slid it under the wooden sides so that all the ground was covered, including around the sides of the bed.

Before we laid any cardboard, weeds such as dandelion, buttercup, and a lot of bindweed were growing in the location of our new bed. Bindweed is the most persistent weed that many of us will encounter, but we did not need to remove any regrowth in the first autumn. That's because bindweed stops growing by October, at about the same time that the cardboard is decomposing, two months after making any bed.

Composting

To fill the bed, we used three different composts, putting the least fertile one on first and the most fertile one at the top. The first layer was green waste compost, started four months earlier. It was well decomposed but would not have many microbes. The second layer was cow manure, purchased two months earlier and containing a bedding of small woodchip. The texture is soft and there is no smell. The top layer was my own compost, nine months old and slightly lumpy with a few woody bits. These were the composts which I happened to have most of at that time, so this is not a strict recipe. You can use any compost to make your no-dig bed.

A really enjoyable part of making a new bed was walking on the compost, once it's all in place. The kids had fun doing this! The whole process was so simple and quick. Within three hours, the children and I had created a bed which was lovely and soft and ready for plants.

Planting

We planted the bed before lunchtime, and that took less than an hour. I used a long-handled wooden dibber to make holes for the seedlings, spaced at nine inches equal distances in all directions.

You can plant a bed with seeds or plants. It's easier and quicker when they are two- to three-week-old plants, rather than sowing seeds. The plants we used had been sown two weeks earlier in my greenhouse.

Aftercare

There are rabbits at Homeacres, and they especially like to eat small seedlings. Therefore, we covered the bed with mesh, supported by wire hoops. The mesh stayed on for four weeks until the plants were big.

It happened to rain a fair amount during the first week after planting, so we did not need to water at all in the first fortnight. In dry weather you need to water new plantings at least twice, until you see strong new growth.

We hardly did any weeding, and that is such a nice part of no-dig. A few weeds did grow through the mulches and we pulled them. There were a few grass seeds in my homemade compost, which are quick and easy to pull when small.

Creating a no-dig bed

The measurements in this project are based on the Homeacres bed from pages 22-23, but you can create a no-dig bed for whatever size space you have.

Where should I put my new bed?

Plants grow in both sunny and shady positions. You will grow the best vegetables and flowers if your bed is in the sun for more than half of the daylight hours. It should not be too shaded by trees, hedges, or buildings. Trees and hedges also send out roots which can suck moisture from your beds.

You can make beds on sloping ground. It works best when beds run up and down a slope, not across it. That means new water and compost run down the length of the whole bed.

Step 1: *Measure an area that is about 4 x 8 feet.*

Step 2: *Lay down wooden planks to act as temporary sides for the new bed. You can remove these once the bed is established and reuse them to create another bed.*

Step 3: *Hammer a couple of wooden battens on the outside of each length of wood to keep them in place. Ideally, the battens should be 12-14 inches long, with a pointed end.*

Step 4: *Place a layer of cardboard on the ground of your new bed, making sure to have removed any tape from the cardboard first. All the edges of the cardboard should be overlapping so that no light is able to get through to the grass or weeds underneath.*

Step 5: *Slide the cardboard under the wooden board so that about 16-18 inches around the edge of the bed is also covered. This stops the weeds from growing back in from the sides.*

Step 6: *Fill the bed with compost. If you have different types of compost, put the least fertile one on first and the most fertile one on top.*

Step 7: *Walk on the compost to press it down. Make sure to push the compost down at the edges of the bed as well. Your new no-dig bed is now ready to be planted!*

Planting a no-dig bed

Sowing and planting are the fun and creative parts once you have your bed in place. Not only will you do a first planting, but you will also do extra planting as soon as spaces appear, after each harvest.

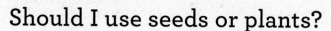

Should I use seeds or plants?

You can either plant seeds, seedlings, or larger plants into your no-dig bed. Quicker harvests come after you set out larger plants rather than sowing seeds directly into the bed. You will use more seed when sowing direct because there is some wastage; not all of them will germinate. A useful and old saying about sowing seeds is:

"One for the rook, one for the crow, one to die, one to grow"

However, this was for wheat sown in big fields, where there was no way to protect seeds from the birds.

Sowing small seeds

You can use almost any tool to draw a narrow line for sowing seeds in the soft surface compost. I often use one or two fingers, pulling them towards me to make a hollow ½ to one inch deep and one inch wide.

If the compost is quite dry, you can help seeds to germinate before you even sow them by carefully dribbling a line of water along the bottom of the hollow you have made. Filling your watering can half full, so it's not too heavy, works well for this.

Now you can sow seeds, according to the time of year and what you want to grow. After sowing, gently pull a little compost from each side of the hollow to make the compost level. In dry weather, use the palm of your hand to flatten the compost and hold moisture.

Sowing large seeds

When sowing larger seeds such as pea, broad bean, and runner beans, you can use a dibber or a similar tool to make holes. Then pop in the seeds and refill the holes with your fingers, using the surrounding compost.

Transplanting

A good first step is to make evenly spaced holes for your seedlings. In the Homeacres bed described on pages 22-23, these holes were spaced nine inches apart. The same spacing was used for all the different vegetables planted. We used a tool called a dibber to make the holes, but you can use a stick to make the holes if you don't have one of those. You can also make your own dibber (see page 41). Place each seedling carefully in its hole, firming the compost around the roots with your hands. You want firm contact between the new plant's roots and the compost of the bed. As well as the gentle push downward, watering helps achieve this.

Watering new plantings

Give your seedlings a light watering, being careful not to swamp them. If plants are close together, water the whole bed. If plants are widely spaced, such as zucchini and tomatoes, use a watering can to give a little water to each new plant. If the weather is dry, make sure to water daily for one or two weeks, until the plants have settled in and put down new roots. You'll know this by noticing how the leaves quite suddenly look darker and are a little larger.

What is a weed?

To call a person or plant a weed is not a compliment. What justification do we have for doing that in a garden? Weeds are plants that are growing naturally and in the wrong place for a gardener. More precisely they are uninvited, fast growing, and quick to spread.

1: Weed plants have little food value although you can eat the leaves of bittercress, fathen, dandelion, and stinging nettle.

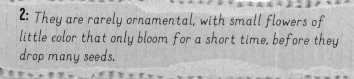

2: They are rarely ornamental, with small flowers of little color that only bloom for a short time, before they drop many seeds.

3: Annual weeds multiply rapidly by seed and then prevent light getting to other plants, such as young vegetable seedlings.

4: Perennial weeds come back every year and spread out to cover large areas that prevent other plants from thriving.

Why do weeds grow?

On a positive note, weeds are healers. Their roots restore structure to broken soil, and their leaves help the surface to stay moist after it has been fragmented and fissured by digging. Weeds do add organic matter to the soil, but annual weeds drop massive numbers of seeds and perennial weeds can completely colonize a planting area and smother the plants that we want to be growing there.

How can I reduce weeds?

The best way to reduce weed numbers is no-dig, because it keeps soil intact and covered by mulch so the weed seeds don't get the light they need to germinate. This state of healthy soil does not need the weeds to help its structure. It grows just a few, perhaps from seeds which have blown in, or from roots of perennial weeds which are already there. It is the soil organisms who enrich soil and improve its structure. It is not the ideal environment for weeds so they don't bother growing.

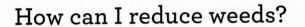

What mulch should I use?

You can use compost at any stage of decomposition, wood chopped into small pieces, or plain brown cardboard with the tape removed. If you are growing vegetables, the best mulch to use is compost. If you have large plants, such as fruit bushes with many weeds growing between them, lay cardboard over the weeds and put woody materials and tree leaves on top.

How can I make weeding fun?

At the Skool Beanz garden patch (page 36), despite all their mulches they still had a very persistent weed growing through. Horsetail (*Equisetum arvense*) pokes up through the ground like pointy witches' fingers. Lara turned the weeding into a game. Each child was given a bucket and a trowel. They had 10 minutes to collect as many weeds as they could. They received a mark out of 10 for number of weeds they can collect and whoever has most points at the end of the season wins a secret prize. This game proved so popular that soon they were running out of horsetail!

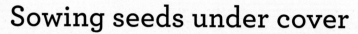

Sowing seeds under cover

Plants want to grow and we just need to understand how best to help them do it. It's remarkable how seeds contain all the information they will need, including the perfect conditions they need to ensure they grow strong.

By understanding this, we can time our planting and increase the success of our sowings. This will depend on where in the world you live, so check your seed packets for the best time to sow (or look at the tables on pages 32, 34, and 35).

Remember that seeds need warmth to germinate. Nature has programmed your seeds to start growing at a certain temperature, to give the plants the maximum chance of survival. Our best way of helping them to grow is to sow seeds in a protected space, which guarantees the appropriate warmth. Early growth is strongest when the plant is under cover, like a greenhouse, an unheated conservatory, or even a window sill, and another positive is that compared to sowing outside, there is usually less pest damage to those young and tender new leaves.

Grow your own cress

Seeds of cress are easy to germinate and fast to grow, even at quite low temperatures. Why not try this experiment in early spring to see how the growth of your seedlings are affected by light, temperature, and weather?

You will need:

Pots to sow seeds in
(yogurt pots are perfect)

Cress seeds

Very fine compost especially for
growing seeds or multi-purpose compost

Notebook and pencil

Step 1: *Fill your pots with compost. If you are using yogurt pots, you will need to punch holes in the bottom for the water to drain away.*

Step 2: *Sprinkle the cress seeds across the top of the soil and water well.*

Step 3: *Put half of your seeds on a sunny windowsill. Put the other half of your seeds outside in the garden.*

Step 4: *Check both of them after 3 days and make a note of your findings, then check the plants daily to see how they grow. How can you use this knowledge to grow other types of plants?*

You will probably see sprouts growing on the pot inside first, because it is warmer indoors and the seedlings are protected. The leaves of the indoor group may appear to be better because they have been protected from the colder weather. The group growing outside will grow more slowly because they are not as warm, but this group will have been grown in full light so they have stronger stems. Full light is not a reference to sunlight, but to light from all directions. If a plant is growing in a window, there is a darker room on one side of it and so it only gets half the light it would get if it were outside. This does not matter for germination but will affect its growth.

Sowing for four seasons of food

Except in winter, sowing seeds happens throughout the year, and there's often time to sow again if you miss the first date. Sowing and planting at any time is easy with no-dig, because your beds are always ready for seeds and plants, without requiring any special preparation. All you need to do is rake the surface to make it level, and remove any weeds.

You can sow seeds from the middle of February (under cover only at that time) to early November. Many vegetables mature in half a year or less, giving you two opportunities for sowing them. Decide what you want to grow, and then match the numbers in the table on pages 34-35 to those on the right, so you know when your harvest is likely to happen. Beetroot is a nice example because it matures quickly from your first sowing, and will be ready in June to August. Then you can sow again in June for harvesting beetroot in autumn, and even into the winter months.

On the following page, I have given each seasonal planting time a number from 1 to 5. Simply match the numbers to the planting chart on page 34 to see what you should plant in which season and when you should expect it to be ready.

Southern Hemisphere

The chart overleaf is for a Northern Hemisphere garden. If you live in the Southern Hemisphere, check the table below for the best dates to plant where you live.

Plants	Sow under cover	Sow outside	Transplant outside
Plants in group 1	September	October	November
Plants in group 2	October	November	December
Plants in group 3	December	January	February
Plants in group 4	February	March	April
Plants in group 5	March	April	May

1: These are EARLY SPRING sowings for harvests in EARLY SUMMER. These are ideal for schools because you can enjoy the harvests before the summer break. If your chosen vegetable is also marked with a 3, sow that vegetable again before leaving for summer, to give you food in autumn.

2: These are MID-SPRING sowings for harvests in SUMMER AND AUTUMN, and perhaps even WINTER. Most of these grow more slowly, and have a long period of harvest at different times.

3: These are EARLY SUMMER sowings for harvests in AUTUMN and perhaps WINTER. From early summer, follow my timings closely. Sowing dates become more precise because we need to make sure that there is sufficient time for plants to crop before winter.

4: These are LATE SUMMER sowings for harvests in AUTUMN AND WINTER. In the rush of summer and when you have lots to eat, make a special note to remember the sowing dates of these vegetables. For schools, sow them as soon as you return, in the first week after summer break.

5: These are AUTUMN sowings for harvests the following year. These vegetables grow slowly and survive winter as small plants, but with a strong root system below ground. Then in spring they grow fast and give nice harvests the following year.

When to sow and plant common vegetables

VEG + timings pp34/5	Sow under cover	Sow outside	Transplant outside
Beetroot 1, 3	March to June	Mid-April to June	April to mid-July
Broad beans 1, 5	Late October to April	Mid-October to May	November to May
Broccoli/calabrese 1,3	March to June	Best not	April to July
Cabbage/cauliflower 1, 2, 3, 4	March to June	Best not	April to July
Carrot 1, 3	Best not	Late March to early July	N/A
Chard 1, 3	April to July	May to July	May to July
Corn 2	Mid-April to May	Mid-to late May	Mid-May to early June
Cucumber ridge 2	June	June	June to early July
French, runner 2	May	June to early July	June to mid-July
Garlic 5	N/A	September to February	N/A
Kale 2, 3	April to July	Best not	May to early August
Leeks 2	April	April	June to July
Lettuce 1, 2, 3	February to July	March to July	March to August
Onions, bulb 1	February to March	March to April	March to April
Parsnips 2	N/A	March to June	N/A

Peas 1	February to May	March to May	March to May
Potato early 1	N/A	March to April	N/A
Potato second, main 2	N/A	April to early May	N/A
Radish 1, 4	February to September	March to September	March to September
Spinach 1, 4	February, March and August	March and August	March and August
Spring onions 1, 2, 4	February to August	March to August	March to September
Squash 2	Mid-April to May	Late May	Late May to early June
Zucchini 2	May	June	Late May to June

Greenhouse/Polytunnel

Two example vegetables	Sow under cover	Transplant under cover
Cucumber cordon 2	Mid-April to mid-May	Mid-May to mid-June
Tomatoes 1	Mid-March to early April	Mid-May to early June

A no-dig sensory garden

Lara Honnor from Skool Beanz Gardening Club

Lara started Skool Beanz to support her community and the children who live there. It's an after-school gardening club and runs every week: the kids, aged 4 to 11, have their own patch. Lara has a Diploma in Social and Therapeutic Horticulture, and uses plants and gardens to improve physical and mental health, communication, and thinking skills.

Making gardening fun and instant is the key to engaging children. It's funny how working with kids teaches us so much. In our Skool Beanz patch, there are areas for cut flowers, fruit, and vegetables, plus a work area with a table, compost bays, rainwater collecting station, and a quiet wildlife garden with pond. There are after-school and Saturday gardening clubs, with the latter running even during school breaks.

At the club, children harvest zucchinis as big as babies, decorate terracotta pots, and excavate potatoes as if looking for dinosaur bones. We trust them with scissors to pick buckets of dahlias to arrange into aluminum can vases.

We focus much of our gardening activity on sensory play, which can come in many forms. A garden provides so many wonderful sensory experiences for children. There is no better place to get completely covered in dirt and soaking wet. Often sensory joy is found in unlikely places.

Touch

While feeding birds, the children plunge their hands into the bag of bird seed up to their armpits and would like to stay that way all day. They love the feel of the seeds and say it feels like sand. They dig their fingers into compost, which feels like a yummy gooey chocolate cake. When watering the plants, children also water each other.

Smell

The children pick bunches of sweet peas and other flowers and breathe in that heavenly scent. They sniff the pungent smell of fresh tomatoes growing on the vine—so much brighter than the smell of store-bought tomatoes.

Sound

Kohlrabi plants look like something from out of space with alien antennas—the children refer to them as "Cool"-rabi. When removing any lower dead and yellowing leaves, it makes a fantastic snapping sound. When harvesting kale, the children push the leaves down at the stem to remove them and that also makes that lovely snap the children can listen out for. The leaves of salad onions make a symphonic squish when you twist them.

Pea shoots make a lovely snappy sound when you pick them, and when pea pods are gone over they crackle when opened, and the hard seeds make that rattling noise when sprinkled on a hard surface.

Sight

When dead-heading flowers, instead of throwing them into the compost, turn them into confetti. On the garden patch the children know to save the best dahlias for vases. But the browning, dying flowers can be cut and the petals picked off to make confetti. The children love immersing their hands into rainbow heaps of petals, sprinkling them onto the tray. At the end of the session, every child takes a handful and on the count of three they throw it up into the air to squeals of delight.

Taste

Each time a new visitor comes to the Skool Beanz garden, one of the children volunteers to give them a guided tour. I have noticed they always make a point of showing them the "pepper flower." This is the name invented by the children for the nasturtium. When I first told them the orange flower is edible and has a peppery flavor they were aghast that a flower could be eaten. But now they take great pride in devouring them in front of new visitors to get a reaction and insist on them having a taste.

Raising seedlings

Small is beautiful! Little pots and module cells are more efficient than the bigger versions. They take up less space on a windowsill or inside a greenhouse. They need only a small amount of compost to fill them and seedlings grow better in the smaller quantities of compost.

Transplant small

As seedlings become young plants, they need increasing space for leaves and roots. It works well to transplant when they are small and young, just two or three weeks old on average. Interestingly there are big advantages to setting out small plants, compared to older large ones.

Options for pots and module trays

You can make your own small pots with two sheets of newspaper, cut to 12 or 16 in. lengths and 1.5 in. wide. Wrap them around and around a small jar of 1 in. diameter, then lightly glue the outer end, and slide off your little pot. Or you can purchase module trays which are easier to fill than the paper pots.

1. Small plants adapt more quickly to their new home.

2. It's quick because the root-holes you make are small, and easy to dib (not dig!).

3. You can grow a lot of plants in a small space, because no plants stay there for long.

Trays of good quality are made with strong plastic, last for decades and are much better value than cheaper, single use plastic trays. Also you get stronger plants because they slide out easily without root damage. If you want a plastic-free alternative, try egg cartons. I sometimes sow peas this way, with two seeds in each partition.

Options for seed trays

The top of the egg carton has no partitions and you can fill it with compost to serve as a seed tray for sowing some small seeds. Sprinkle them on top of the compost and then water lightly, and it's best usually not to cover with more compost. Just lay a clear plastic bag on top of the tray to retain moisture, until you see the first tiny leaves after 5-7 days. The first roots from small seeds are fragile, and you could add 50% vermiculite to the compost, an expanded rock which is very light and holds air, which makes it easier for the first tiny roots to grow.

Watering

Little roots risk rotting if their compost is soggy; always be careful not to overwater. Preferably the compost will look a little dry on top before you water, especially in winter, when growth is so slow and the air is already humid or moist.

Upcycling in the garden
Lara and Charles

Reusing stuff is fun and is more eco-friendly even than recycling, because there is no industrial process needed to remake materials into a new product. You're just doing subtle conversions for a change of use.

Can vases

With some old baked bean aluminum cans, wondrous things can happen. Any aluminum can will do; just remove the labels, wash them or pop them in the dishwasher, and they come out sparkling. Children take great joy in decorating them with acrylic pens—rainbow stripes are always a favorite. Be careful of the sharpness where the lid was removed and always tell them not to touch the inside of the can, and to be extra safe you can line the top with masking tape. Let them fill the vases with a watering can and choose their flowers from the garden. Show them how to remove the lower leaves and let them cut the stem to size. They can then leave a vase on each doorstep around the garden patch to cheer up the local residents! In this picture (left) we have used them as a temporary home for some indoor plants.

Old boot pots

If a hole appears in your rubber boot then it is the perfect excuse to turn it into a plant pot. When I arrived to take a school gardening session with a trash bag full of old boots and a tray of bright yellow marigolds the children thought I was nuts. Anything that can hold compost and can have a hole drilled in the bottom to let water out can be made into a plant pot. There were plenty of giggles as they decorated their boots with acrylic pens and squished handfuls of compost and marigolds into them and they brought even more cheer to the playground all lined up against the wall.

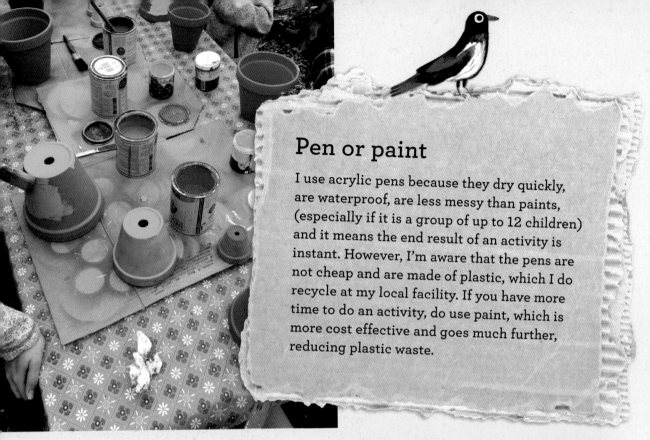

Pen or paint

I use acrylic pens because they dry quickly, are waterproof, are less messy than paints, (especially if it is a group of up to 12 children) and it means the end result of an activity is instant. However, I'm aware that the pens are not cheap and are made of plastic, which I do recycle at my local facility. If you have more time to do an activity, do use paint, which is more cost effective and goes much further, reducing plastic waste.

Make your own dibber

You may well have an old and unwanted tool lying around, perhaps that rusty old spade which you now don't need for digging! Most old tools still have decent wooden handles, which you can remove from the iron part and convert into a long-handled dibber, for making holes when planting. If the handle is longer than you feel comfortable using, first cut it to length. Then use a saw to cut triangular wedges off the bottom end and make it more pointed, but not with a long point. It works best with a round and blunt end, so that the hole it makes in compost does not have a long, thin, and unused space below your new plants' roots, when you pop them in. After using the saw to round the bottom end, some edges will be jagged and quite sharp. Use rough sandpaper to smooth them a lot, and then the dibber slides easily into and out of a bed, making a neat hole without disturbing much of the surface.

Attract wildlife to your garden

Much of what we call wildlife is too small to see, and keeps out of our way, or comes out at night. If we could see microscopically and in the dark, we would be more amazed at the riches of nature.

"Wild" usually refers to plants and places which have not been changed by us! It is about animals, insects, and plants which arrive and live their lives without our help. So you could say that a wild garden is a really easy one. The snag is it might grow plants you don't want like brambles and stinging nettles, and then you can't get out there to enjoy it.

Nothing exists without eating and there is a pyramid of eaters and those who are eaten, below and above the soil. Creatures like springtails, a fraction of an inch long, eat decaying leaves and fungi, while they get eaten by ants and spiders. Higher up the food chain are woodlice, centipedes, millipedes, earthworms, slugs, and birds. All this amazing life can prosper and multiply when there are two things: food and somewhere to live.

Most wildlife lives close to the surface of the soil. We can create habitats for them to live in by simply leaving a piece of wood or flat stone lying on the ground, whether on grass or bare soil. Leave it overnight and lift it up again in the morning. Look out for collembola, with six legs, two antenna, and a habit of jumping in the air. They occur in many shapes, sizes, and colors and some are truly beautiful with faces and big eyes. These tiny creatures are not considered insects because a collembola's mouth is inside their body. An insect's mouth is outside their body!

Small piles of wood and leaves can attract bumblebees. Mark your pile with a stick so that it doesn't get tidied up by mistake. There is no need to buy expensive "bug hotels" in the stores when your garden can provide fantastic, natural, and free materials. Try bits of hollow bamboo canes, corrugated cardboard, woodchip, and bark. Your own imagination and a few tools are all you need to make something beautiful for your garden that wildlife will love!

How can we help?

We start with the soil of course! We add compost and organic matter on top, and that's a feast right there. Then, through no-dig, we give space for the wildlife to live and thrive. We keep intact the homes of billions of organisms, and when they eat and multiply, there is food for all, including us, through the successful growth of plants.

School gardens in Surrey, England
Joe Sparks from The Green Room Schools

Joe is founder and CEO of The Green Room schools which include a no-dig market garden for students to grow, manage, harvest, and sell food. The money they make goes to a school in Ghana.

Growing food is fun and no-dig is a new way of doing it. The children like to be curious and no-dig helps them to learn through discovery. We can keep our gardening simple and we can focus on food growing. We keep experimenting and are not afraid to make mistakes—even our mistakes are delicious! You can grow alongside your plants and discover every day what makes this so magical.

Here are Joe's top tips for having more to eat, while helping nature.

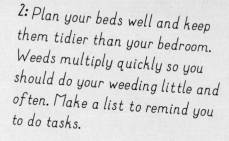

1: Keep it simple! All you need to start your no-dig garden is cardboard, compost, a rake, and a dibber.

2: Plan your beds well and keep them tidier than your bedroom. Weeds multiply quickly so you should do your weeding little and often. Make a list to remind you to do tasks.

3: Worms are our friends: give them stuff to eat and they do the rest. Treat your garden like a vegetable safari, and watch the wildlife with wonder.

4: All weather is good weather. Love the light, love the dark, love the misty, windy, cloudy days, and the sunny, balmy ones. There are four seasons of growth and harvests, including winter when you can go and pick from your garden fridge!

5: Cook what you grow and even what you don't know. Our students feed themselves and our schools too! They work alongside our school chefs and learn to cook exciting dishes with the produce they grow.

Grow a giant sunflower

Giant sunflowers are quick and easy to grow and are a great way to get children interested in caring for their own plants. Make sure that the seed packet tells you which type of sunflower you are sowing. You want to choose one that's described as a tall variety with a single stem. The seeds are medium sized and easy to sow.

You will need:

- Plant pots (2 in. and 4 in.)
- Some reasonably fine compost
- Sunflower seeds

Step 1: *Fill each pot with the compost and make a small hole in the center with your finger or the blunt end of a pencil, no more than ½ cm deep.*

Step 2: *Drop a single seed into each pot and cover them over with the compost.*

Step 3: *Water well.*

Step 4: *You now need to keep your seeds in a warm place for about a week to help them to germinate. You can even put them in a dark cupboard if that's the warmest place. The seeds do not need light to germinate, just temperatures above about 68°F (20°C) for the first five days or so.*

Step 5: *Once you see the first little leaf popping up, the plants need light. They don't need it to be so warm now but keep them in a place where the temperature is about 59°F (15°C). The little seedlings also must never freeze or they will die, and this is why we sow in May rather than April. You could sow in early June, this just means there is less time for the plants to grow tall.*

Step 6: *When your plants are 3 to 4 in. high, it's time for them to move into a larger 4 in. pot with some fresh compost. Be very gentle when you tap out the rootball from the small pot. They will stay in these new pots until they are ready to be planted outside.*

Step 7: *When they get to 6 to 8 in. tall, they are ready to move to their final spot in the garden. You may need a stick and a string tie to support them at first. It helps to bury some of the stem below soil level when you transplant them. Soon they develop woody stems which are strong and don't blow over.*

Step 8: *Your plant will stop growing taller when it starts to grow petals, soon after midsummer.*

Collecting seeds for next year

If the weather is warm in late summer, the flower may develop seeds that you can save for next year. By early autumn there will be a mass of seeds with pointed ends sticking outward, under a dark layer of old petals which you can rub off. Look closely to see the beautiful spiral of seed development from the center. Have you spotted anything else in nature with this vortex pattern? It goes to the heart of how plants grow, and reveals the incredible intelligence wrapped up in nature around us.

Top Tip

One way to grow tall sunflowers is to deprive them of some light. Try growing a very tall sunflower against a wall. This makes the plant grow upwards in search of light, but it also makes the stems weaker and thinner, so they may need support all the time, especially if it's a windy spot.

Grow and carve a Halloween pumpkin

With a bit of planning ahead, you can grow your own pumpkin that will be ready to harvest at Halloween. Make sure you choose a variety that is larger in size as they have softer skins. The seed packet will tell you how big your pumpkin could grow. The ultimate size depends on summer weather and how much space you give it. Like sunflowers, it is best to sow your pumpkin seeds in late April or early May under glass or on a windowsill. Then you will have a strong plant by the end of May. Pumpkin seeds are large and grow fast in warmth so there is no advantage from sowing too early.

You will need:

- Pots of between 3 and 4 in.
- Pumpkin seeds
- A space under glass or a windowsill

Step 1: *Fill the pot with compost. Make a small hole in the middle of the compost with your finger or with the blunt end of a pencil, and drop a single seed into the hole. Cover it over with the compost and water well. Place it in a bright, warm place. You should have a nice strong plant in about 4 weeks.*

Step 2: *Once the risk of frost at night is gone, your pumpkin can be planted in your garden. If you are growing more than one pumpkin, you need to plant each one at least three feet apart. If you want really big pumpkins, they could have up to 10 feet of space for each plant.*

Step 3: *To discourage weeds from growing around your pumpkins, lay overlapping cardboard on the soil around the plants and hold down the corners with large stones. The bugs will love living under this!*

Step 4: *During warm weather in June and July the plants grow very fast and fill all the space, with enormous leaves. At first you will see only leaves. Then in August as they start to die back and have white mildew on them (which is quite normal), the fruits are suddenly noticeable. If it does not rain much and the weather is hot, it's worth giving some water, mainly in July.*

Step 5: *Pumpkins are ready to harvest once the leaves have mostly died away, from the end of September and into October.*

Top tip

When you are cutting your pumpkin free, take care not to knock off the stalk because they will then not keep very well. I recommend that you cut the softer, trailing stem on either side of the stalk and then you can pick up your pumpkins. Bring them into any warm room so that the skins can dry, then they will keep well. Once you cut into the skin in order to carve, the flesh will start to decay and you will need to eat them up in a few days. Large pumpkins are good for making soup, and smaller varieties are delicious roasted. Don't forget to save a few seeds for next year's pumpkin!

Vegetables need company!

Plants feel things. They grow better for us when we treat them with love and respect. In return they grow a warm and healthy look to their leaves which we find pleasing. Like people, plants enjoy company, especially when young and small.

To see how much companion planting can benefit your plants, why not try this experiment.

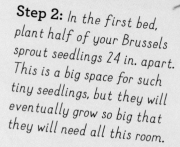

YOU WILL NEED:
Brussels sprout seedlings
Lettuce seedlings

Step 1: Prepare two beds.

Step 2: In the first bed, plant half of your Brussels sprout seedlings 24 in. apart. This is a big space for such tiny seedlings, but they will eventually grow so big that they will need all this room.

Step 3: In the second bed plant the other half of the Brussels sprout seedlings at the same distance of 24 in. apart but this time plant a lettuce seedling in between each space.

Step 4: Check them weekly and make a note of which bed grows the biggest plants. You can use this knowledge to improve your crop next year.

Let's be friends!

Broccoli and lettuce grow well together because they are ready to harvest at different times. By the time the broccoli needs the space that the lettuce is taking up, the lettuce will be ready to pick. Planting different varieties of plants together can help them grow up to 50% bigger than if they were growing alone. You can use this method to grow lots of different plants like . . .

. . . broccoli and cilantro . . .

. . . corn with one pumpkin. . .

. . . and lettuce with tomato.

A no-dig market garden
Johanna Kispel and her children at Long Orchard

Johanna started a no-dig garden in 2019 with her children, who are calm when in the garden and love having compost on their hands. During the 2020 lockdown, people were eager to buy her produce and plants at the local market. Somehow Johanna finds time for all this on top of working at the local hospital. Here's what she has to say . . .

Growing food is fun and no-dig is a new way of doing it. The children like to be curious and no-dig helps them to learn through discovery. We can keep our gardening simple and we can focus on food growing. We keep experimenting and are not afraid to make mistakes—even our mistakes are delicious! You can grow alongside your plants and discover every day what makes this so magical.

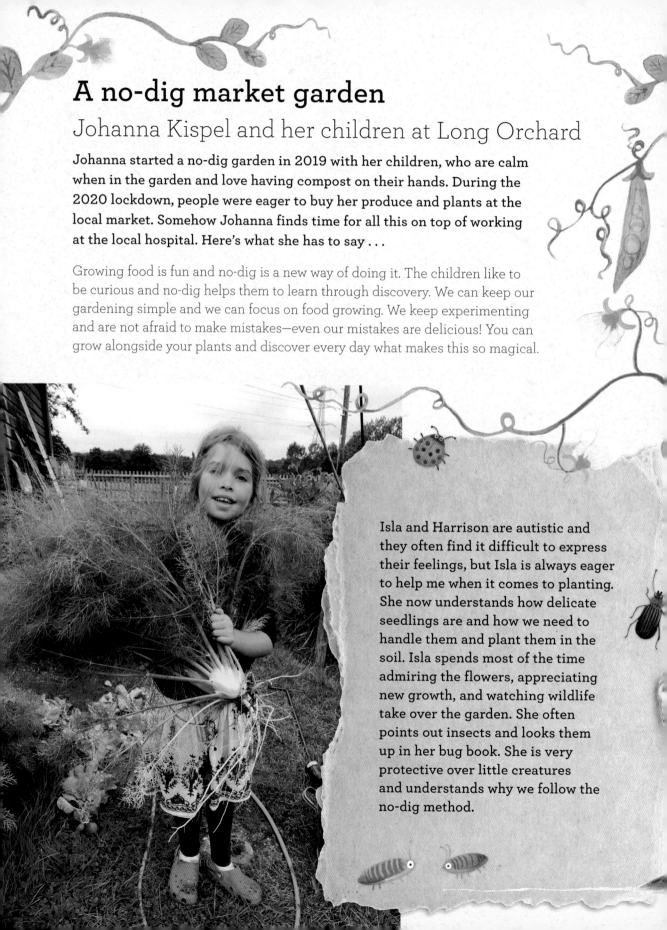

Isla and Harrison are autistic and they often find it difficult to express their feelings, but Isla is always eager to help me when it comes to planting. She now understands how delicate seedlings are and how we need to handle them and plant them in the soil. Isla spends most of the time admiring the flowers, appreciating new growth, and watching wildlife take over the garden. She often points out insects and looks them up in her bug book. She is very protective over little creatures and understands why we follow the no-dig method.

Harrison is great at helping with the practical tasks such as filling up a bed with compost and clearing weeds. We have also created a digging corner where he is allowed to dig. He absolutely loves the feeling of fresh earth and getting stuck in it.

Isla and Harrison get very excited when friends come around and they can show them their garden and how things grow. This year we created a new area, where peas and strawberries grow. At the beginning of the season they start picking the pea shoots, which are great in salads, and later on they enjoy picking and eating the pea pods.

From March to October I sell the surplus vegetables and seedlings at farmers' markets and car trunk sales. Early on Sunday mornings the whole family gets together to harvest all the vegetables and load them into the trailer. I often sell out at the market, so Dudley and the kids bring more vegetables on a garden trolley, and then help me at the market. It's a great experience for the children to see their work in the garden coming full circle, from planting seeds to eating and selling their own produce. The garden is hugely positive for the children. It helps them to concentrate, manage their feelings, and develop responsibility for the plants.

Be a garden scientist

You don't need a white coat and a laboratory to do amazing experiments. Your garden is the perfect place to study nature and discover ways you can help it grow. So let's go outside!

Do plants know our thoughts?

Can we affect the way our plants grow by mind power? Try this experiment and see for yourself.

Step 1: *You will need two plants of the same size and type.*

Step 2: *Fill two bottles with water and stick a label on each bottle. On one label, write I love you. On the label of the other bottle, write I don't care about you. Leave the bottles for 48 hours.*

Step 3: *Water one plant with the bottle that is labelled I love you. The other plant will be watered by the I don't care about you bottle. Refill the bottles when you have watered the plants.*

Step 4: *Repeat the experiment every week for a month. Record the growing of each plant each week. Do you think your thoughts have made a difference to the plants?*

Can you make your tomatoes sweeter?

How much can we affect the sweetness of vegetables by watering more or less?

Step 1: *Take two tomato plants of the same variety, 6 to 8 in. high in late May. Plant each in a pot of 4 to 5 in. diameter, with multipurpose or potting compost.*

Step 2: *Water normally until August, and then choose one of the plants and give it only half the amount of water you give to the other.*

Step 3: *Record your findings in a notebook. Which plant grows bigger? Which has the biggest tomatoes? Which plant grows tomatoes with the sweetest flavor?*

You can also try this experiment on different kinds of plants such as carrots and see if you get the same result.

Do they want to grow together?

A lettuce heart is the sweetest and most delicious leaves of your plant so how can we help these grow big and strong? Do lettuce closely planted together make the best hearts? Does space affect the health of the leaves?

Step 1: *Take 24 lettuce seedlings, each with two or three leaves. Separate them into three groups, each with eight plants. Group 1 should be planted 4 in. apart. Group 2 should be planted 8 in. Group 3 has the most space, at 12 in. apart.*

Step 2: *Every week check and record the growth of each group. Make a note of the day when the leaves of each plant begin to touch their neighbor. How does this affect their growth? Which group grew the lettuces with the nicest hearts?*

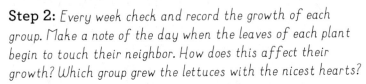

Step 3: *Remember to harvest your lettuce hearts when they feel firm and before the center leaves start to rot.*

Ten easy flowers
(for us and for wildlife)

A few brightly colored flowers look fantastic in all gardens. Here are some of my favorites for you to try in your garden. Many are small plants and you can dot them around, or group them together.

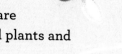

Cornflower, *Centaurea cyanus*, annual • 12 in.

Sow early spring for tall thin plants with pretty flowers through early summer. It will drop its seeds again in September. This is called self-seeding.

Cranesbill, *Geranium pratense*, perennial • 8 in.

Sow or plant in spring for blue and purple flowers all summer, and the leaves attract butterfly larvae. This plant will often self-seed.

Evening primrose, *Oenothera biennis*, biennial • 8 in.

From spring these grow up to three feet tall and flower pale yellow through summer. Flowers are fragrant in evening time and attract moths at night, while birds will enjoy eating the seeds.

Fennel, *Foeniculum vulgare*, perennial • 14 in.

This is a large plant with bronze or green leaves. It seeds in the autumn, after flowering all summer. The seeds can be used in cooking and are also a great source of food for visiting birds.

Foxglove, *Digitalis purpurea*, biennial • 10 in.

Sow early spring for these tall thin plants with pretty flowers through early summer. It will drop its seeds again in September.

Forget-me-not, *Myosotis arvensis*, annual • 4 in.

Fast growing from seed, from spring to midsummer, these tiny blue flowers are bright, pretty, and last well in damp weather, then become clusters of seeds.

Honesty, *Lunaria annual*, biennial • 8 in.

Sow in summer for purple flowers early next spring on stems up to three feet high. The seedpods are beautiful envelopes of transparent material, draped like ghostly silver coins.

Poached egg flower, *Limnanthes douglasii*, annual • 6 in.

The flowers look like poached eggs! These plants flower for a long period, and drop many seeds. After one sowing in spring, you probably won't need to sow again.

Primrose, *Primula vulgaris*, perennial • 4 in.

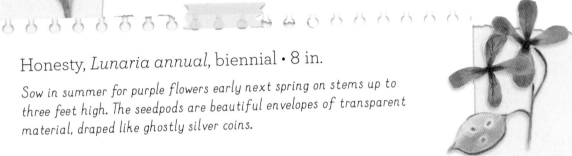

Plant these in the autumn for flowers early in the spring. These are low-growing plants that do well in shade or sun, and they like moisture.

Wallflower, *Erysimum cheiri*. Naturalized, short-lived perennial • 4 in.

True to their name, these grow in stone walls, and also in good soil. Sow summer and plant autumn, for spring flowers of many colors, beautifully scented and liked by insects.

Gardening for children with additional needs

Toni and Tom Hallett

Having children with additional needs, like ADHD (Attention Deficit Hyperactivity Disorder) or autism, makes it a struggle to find family activities that we can enjoy together. We all love nature and we wanted to teach our children how to care for a garden. We wanted them to learn where food comes from, and how to grow it in a safe way with no pesticides. The no-dig method is a perfect fit for us. With the children's help we converted our front yard into a garden, where we have already spent two happy years.

The beauty of the no-dig method for children is its simplicity. Few rules means children enjoy gardening without the fear of getting it wrong. Gardening appeals to all the senses; the visual nature of a garden, from the different colored vegetables and flowers to watching water flow from a watering can.

Children delight in the beautiful world a garden creates, particularly one in harmony with nature. They enjoy watching the different insects and wildlife, and making a game out of what we can hear. They enjoy eating the food that they have grown and are more willing to try new things.

Here are Toni's top tips for gardening as a family.

1: Maintain distinct spaces. Give the children their space to play, but also be clear that they cannot go into the no-dig garden without you. Have it close to the house.

2: Keep gardening times short and sweet.

3: Start with a small area and expand. Make just one bed to start with.

4: Create an area for propagation that the children cannot enter alone, but they can help to look after.

5: Keep your tools at hand and have a water source nearby.

6: Think outside the box. If your child hates getting dirty, use gloves or an apron. In time they will become more tolerant of a bit of dirt.

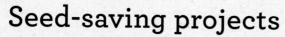

Seed-saving projects
Lara and Charles

Seeds are a fun harvest, a great way to save money—and often the vegetables or flowers from home-saved seeds are healthier and stronger! Make your own seed packets and decorate the labels. They also make lovely gifts.

"Our seed saving is not planned. I have seen 6-year-olds sit quietly for an hour podding: broad beans, sweet peas, and broccoli seeds. Summer sweet peas climb up an arch on the garden patch and the children pick bunches and bunches every week. We let the flowers go to seed and by autumn have plenty of brown seed pods to sort."

Lara, Skool Beanz

Make your own seed packets

Making seed packets is fun, and a way to upcycle old garden catalogs and magazines.

You will need:
- Scrap paper or old magazines
- Seeds
- Colored pencils
- Sticky label or paperclip

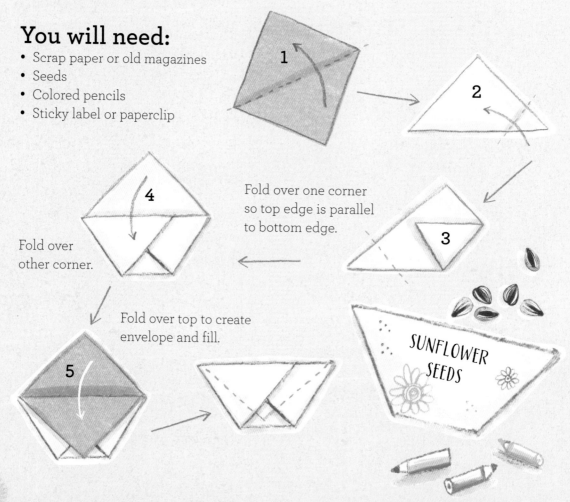

1

2

Fold over one corner so top edge is parallel to bottom edge.

3

4

Fold over other corner.

Fold over top to create envelope and fill.

5

SUNFLOWER SEEDS

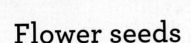

Flower seeds

It's not just seeds in pods that can be saved. We can also save the seeds of our favorite flowers and make sure we can enjoy them year after year.

Poppy

Carefully cut a small hole in the shell of the pretty round seed head. It is filled with lots and lots of tiny black seeds which can be stored safely for next year.

Sunflower

Have fun removing seeds from the big flower heads. For sowing next spring, keep them as you find them. If you want to eat the sunflower seeds you need to extract them from the outer shell. This is a rather tricky job and is best done by gently rolling over them with a pestle in a circular motion until the shell separates from the seed inside.

Marigold

Pull the dead flower from the stem and lots of long black spiky seeds are ready for saving.

Borlotti beans

Wait for the outer shell to go brown and mostly dry, and then remove the hard beans inside. After drying thoroughly in a warm sunny room, store in a jar for cooking.

Pumpkins

Easy to save, just remove them before cooking. Beware! If the flowers have cross-pollinated with a different type of pumpkin or squash growing nearby, this can affect the growth of the new plant.

Tomatoes

Scoop out the seeds from inside a tomato and put them in a cup with water. Leave for a week to go moldy, then scrape off the rotting tomato and rinse the now-clean seeds. These will germinate more strongly because the rotting tomato you removed contains a germination inhibitor.

Useful information

I get my module trays from
www.containerwise.co.uk in the UK.
If you are in North America,
www.allaboutthegarden.com

For compost, do a search for your local
supplier. These often come in plastic-free
reusable bags but transport fees can be
expensive. Why not share the cost with
some local gardeners?

Woodchip can be sourced
for free from a local tree
surgeon. You should also
look for places in the garden
where wood can be left to
decompose.

For potting compost, try your local
garden center or DIY store. Potting
compost is expensive so don't use it for
creating new beds.

Polytunnels make a huge difference both to
what you can grow, and when you can garden.

For plant covers including fleece, mesh and bird netting, visit **www.gardening-naturally.com**

If you need a wooden dibber, don't buy. Make your own from the handle of a broken tool (see page 41) or even a sturdy piece of stick will do the job.

Seeds can be collected from your plants, swapped with other gardeners, or collected from the hedgerow or a forgotten piece of wild ground. There are lots of seed companies that sell a vast range of plant varieties, including unusual vegetables. For wildflower seeds, I recommend making sure they're native to your region.

Please check out my website **www.charlesdowding.co.uk** for details of online courses and products. I sell a handy planting wallchart through my website **www.charlesdowding.com**. There are also loads of how-to videos on my YouTube channel so please do pop by and give me a like. You can also check out another of my books *No-Dig Gardening* (Dorling Kindersley) for more information on the topics found here.

Index